WILLKOMMEN

Dorothea Hamm, Klaus Wagener, Floristmeister vom BLOOM's VIEW-Team.

Dorothea Hamm, Klaus Wagener, master florists of the BLOOM's VIEW team.

Liebe BLOOM's VIEW-Leserinnen und -Leser,

ungewöhnliche Hochzeitslocations mit besonderer Ausstrahlung bestimmen nach wie vor den Trend bei Hochzeitsfeierlichkeiten. Ein Umfeld mit Bezug zu einer bemerkenswerten Vergangenheit oder mit großer Natürlichkeit und in einer nahezu dramatisch wirkenden Landschaft, immer aber mit einer Atmosphäre der Ungezwungenheit, sind Beispiele. Die Kunst der Floraldesigner, die solche Hochzeiten blumig ausrichten, besteht dann darin, ein Gestaltungskonzept im Einklang mit diesen Gegebenheiten zu entwickeln, farblich, formal und vor allem im Style. Dafür bietet die vorliegende Ausgabe eine Fülle an Beispielkreationen von der Feier am Flussufer bis zur Heidehochzeit.

Den je Thema auf meist nur wenige Werkstückbeispiele begrenzten Teil der Hochzeitsgalerie führen wir mit 21 jahreszeitlich geordneten Beiträgen fort, als variantenreichen Beratungsteil für Ihre Kundengespräche mit den Brautleuten. Im Service-Teil vervollständigen Listungen der Werkstoffe und Materialien sowie einige beispielhafte Preis- bzw. Kalkulationsangaben das Themenspektrum.

Wir wünschen Ihnen viel Erfolg in der neuen Hochzeitssaison!

Find us on f
www.facebook.com/bloomspro

Find us on f
www.facebook.com/bloomsworld

Welcome
Dear BLOOM's VIEW reader,

The latest trend for wedding celebrations is still towards unusual wedding locations with special impact. Some examples: surroundings with a remarkable history or locations with distinctly natural flair and an almost dramatic landscape, but in any case with a relaxed atmosphere. The challenge for the floral designer organizing the flowers for such weddings is to develop a concept that is in tune with these surroundings in terms of colour, form and especially style. This issue provides plenty of exemplary designs, from celebrations at the riverside to heather weddings outdoors.

The wedding gallery offers only few workpiece examples per theme with a total of 21 articles sorted by season, which will provide many variations for your customer consultations with bridal couples. The service section completes the theme spectrum with lists of the materials used as well as some example prices and calculations.

We wish you much success in the new wedding season!

Dorothea Hamm Klaus Wagener

& das gesamte BLOOM's VIEW-Team
& the entire BLOOM's VIEW team

WILLKOMMEN

WEDDING

INHALT

HOCHZEITSAUTOS

THEMENHOCHZEITEN

REPORTAGE

HOCHZEITSGALERIE

HOCHZEITSGALERIE ◎ WEDDING GALLERY

View

HOCHZEITSGALERIE

Im Folgenden finden Sie eine Vielzahl von Ideen zu thematisch und saisonal unterschiedlich ausgerichteten Hochzeitsfeiern. Ausgewählte Werkstücke zeigen exemplarisch, wie der Style, die Farbgebung oder der Umgang mit den Blumen gedacht ist. Viele der Brautsträuße sind auf Brautstraußhalter gearbeitet, dies hat den Vorteil der schnelleren und damit preisgünstigeren Erstellung. Oder die Brautsträuße sind mit Naturstielen gebunden. Die damit einhergehende natürlich-unkomplizierte Wirkung bräutlichen Floralschmucks liegt nach wie vor im Trend.

Die Werkstoff- und Materiallistungen finden Sie ab Seite 124. Einige der Werkstücke sind mit Preisangaben versehen, die nicht als absolut zu verstehen sind. Die Preise sind nach unseren Einkaufslisten und Arbeitszeiten kalkuliert worden und können regional und saisonal bedingt bis zu 30 % in beide Richtungen abweichen.

ROMANTISCH
54 Betörender Freesienduft
84 Blütenweiß und Rosarot
120 Winterblühende Purpur-Lenzrose
122 Wünsche werden wahr

VERTRÄUMT
58 Himmelblaue Perlhyazinthen
60 Trauung mit Tulpen
94 Rosencharme in zartem Pastell

LÄNDLICH
64 Frühlingsbunt zur Grünen Hochzeit
104 Dahlien in feurigem Rot
108 Heiraten in der Herbstsonne

PURISTISCH
66 Verführerische Duftnarzissen
98 Kombination von Blütenkuppeln

NOSTALGISCH
70 Romantischer Wickencharme
78 Symbolhafte Brautschmuckringe
90 Sonnengelb auf Hochzeitsreise
112 Hochzeit zur Hagebuttenzeit

KLASSISCH
74 Bräutliche Bouvardien
80 Prunkende Blütenherzen
102 Prunkvoll gefüllte Lilie

EXTRAVAGANT
86 Brautschmuck in Blattmanschette
116 Südafrikanische Brautschmuckexotik

GALERIE

52

WEDDING GALLERY

On the following pages you will find a lot of ideas for differently themed wedding celebrations. Select workpieces show examples of our suggestions about style, colour and construction techniques. Many of the bridal bouquets are based on bouquet holders, which not only save time but also offer a cost-effective advantage. Or the bridal bouquets are hand-tied with natural stems. This natural look is still very much en vogue in wedding design at the moment.

You can find the lists of florals and materials on page 124 ff. Some of the workpieces are priced, but these prices are not intended as absolute figures. The prices are calculated according to our procurement lists and worktime and can deviate up to +/- 30 % due to regional and seasonal factors.

ROMANTIC
54 Enchanting freesia scent
84 Lily white and rosy red
120 Winter blooming hellebores in purple
122 Dreams come true

DREAMY
58 Sky-blue grape hyacinths
60 Tulip wedding
94 Rose charm in pale pastels

COUNTRY
64 Spring colours for a green wedding
104 Dahlias in fiery red
108 Wedding in the autumn sun

PURISTIC
66 Enticingly fragrant daffodils
98 Combination of floral domes

NOSTALGIC
70 Youthful sweet pea charm
78 Symbolic floral rings
90 Sunny yellow honeymoon
112 Wedding in rose hip season

CLASSIC
74 Bridal Bouvardia
80 Resplendent floral hearts
102 Magnificent double lilies

EXTRAVAGANT
86 Bridal designs in leafy collars
116 South African wedding design

53

CONTENTS

WEDDING CARS

THEMED WEDDINGS

REPORT

WEDDING GALLERY

2017

POMPONS & CO.

Pompons, Wimpelketten und andere Dekorationsartikel aus Papier und Stoff sind als Raumschmuck nach wie vor gefragt. Die im Vergleich zu ihrer plakativen Wirkung unaufwändigen Artikel können zudem immer wieder neu verwendet werden.

TISCHSCHMUCK IM BOHO-STYLE

Wie selbstgemacht muss Tischschmuck wirken, wenn er zu einer Hochzeit im angesagten Boho-Style passen soll. Hier sind unkonventionelle Vorgehensweisen, das Integrieren von Alltäglichem wie Flaschen sowie Dekorationselemente, die plakativ das Motto transportieren, genau richtig. Insofern passt der Tischschmuck im Gewächshaus bei unseren Hochzeitsschmuckideen im Vintage-Style auch zu dieser stilistischen Ausrichtung.

STI(E)L ZEIGEN

Angesagt ist zurzeit bei der Brautstraußherstellung die Technik des Bindens mit Naturstielen. Das wirkt unkompliziert, locker und charmant. Ganz so unkompliziert ist es aber nicht, will man fachlich korrekt arbeiten. **Das Problem:**
Offene, womöglich noch feuchte Schnittstellen mit austretendem Pflanzensaft können das Brautkleid beschädigen. Neben der entsprechenden Trageberatung für solch einen Brautstrauß sind das **die Lösungen:**

- sicherstellen, dass Stiele und Stielenden vollkommen trocken sind.
- die Stielenden mit Stoff- oder Bandumwicklungen kaschieren.
- die Stielenden in flüssiges, weißes Kerzenwachs eintauchen.

Teelichtwachs ist ungeeignet, da es relativ weich bleibt und fettet.

LIEBENSWERT: BLUSHING BRIDE

Am südafrikanischen Kap blüht von Juli bis Oktober diese Schönheit aus der Familie der Proteaceen: *Serruria florida*. Besonders liebenswert ist der zarte Hauch von Rosa, der die Blütenstände überzieht und ihr den englischen Namen eingebracht hat, der „Errötende Braut" bedeutet. Perfekte Schmuckblüte für eine Braut am Beginn der kalten Jahreszeit.

1. Pompom & Co. Pompoms, bunting and other deco articles made of paper and fabric are ever-popular as room decorations. So easy to make and yet full of eye-catching impact, they can also be reused in different ways.

2. Boho table deco. Table decorations must have a homemade look if they are to go with a bohemian-style wedding. Unconventional approaches, integrating everyday items and eye-catching deco elements are just the ticket. The table decorations in the greenhouse in our vintage wedding deco ideas are a perfect match for this style orientation.

3. Stems in style. Today many bridal bouquets use the tying technique with natural stems, although cut stems could leak and stain the wedding dress. To prevent this, the stems are allowed to dry completely and then sealed at the ends with candle wax and/or wrapped in ribbon. In general, the bride will be advised as to how to carry such a bouquet.

4. Blushing Bride. From July through October, a protea beauty blooms along the South African Cape: *Serruria florida*. Particularly appealing is the hint of pink that tinges its flowers and gives this perfect bridal flower its English name.

HOCHZEITS-TRENDS 2017

Was ist neu? Was bleibt? Wir fragten Redakteurin Lale Akarsu aus der Redaktion des Hochzeitsmagazins Braut & Bräutigam und bekamen die folgenden Trendhinweise:

BLÜTEN ZUR HOCHZEITSTORTE.

Selbstverständlich werden nur Blüten verwendet, die essbar sind oder keine Geschmacks- bzw. Duftstoffe an die Torte abgeben und aus biologischem Anbau stammen. **(→ S. 25 f.)**

PANTONE®
15-0343 TCX
Greenery

GREENERY – DIE NEUE FARBE.

Wichtigste Farbe für 2017 ist der Pantone-Ton „Greenery". Er symbolisiert im Brautschmuck Natürlichkeit und Hoffnung. **(→ S. 86 ff., S. 98 ff.)**

Außerdem im Trend: Farbverläufe in der Art von Ombré **(→ S. 46 ff., S. 54 ff., S. 120 ff.)** sowie der Aquarell-Look mit pastelligen Farben bei Blumenschmuck, Torten und Papeterie. **(→ S. 6 ff., S. 16 ff., S. 32 ff., S. 70 ff., 94 ff.)**

BOHO- UND ETHNO-STYLE TOTAL BELIEBT!

Der Ausdruck einer ungezwungen-lockeren Leichtigkeit gehört zum Lebensgefühl der Brautleute unverzichtbar dazu. Der passende Brautstrauß entsteht in einfacher Bindetechnik. Perfekte Ergänzungen: Federn, Gräser und lange Bänder, die die Blüten umspielen und leicht im Wind flattern. **(→ S. 16 ff., S. 54 ff., S. 64 f., S. 116 f.)**

SONNENGESICHTIGE BLÜTEN ABSOLUT „IN"!

Ihre charmant-schlichte Erscheinung ist ein Ausdruck von Harmonie und guter Laune par excellence, also wie geschaffen für die Brautfloristik. **(→ Seite 90 ff.)**

Wedding trends 2017

What's new? What stays? We asked Lale Akarsu, editor of wedding magazine "Braut & Bräutigam", and got the following trend tips:

1. Flowers and floral garlands for the wedding cake. Naturally, only flowers are used which are edible or don't add any flavour or fragrance to the cake. They should also stem from organic cultivation. **(→ p. 25 f.)**

2. Greenery – the new shade. The most important colour for 2017 is Pantone "Greenery". In bridal decorations it symbolizes naturalness and hope. **(→ p. 86 ff., p. 98 ff.)** Also in trend: colour gradations in the ombré style **(→ p. 46 ff., p. 54 ff., p. 120 ff.)** and aquarelle effects with pastel shades for floral decorations, cakes and paper elements. **(→ p. 6 ff., p. 16 ff., p. 32 ff., p. 70 ff., p. 94 ff.)**

3. Boho and ethno absolute favourites! Expressing an informal and relaxed lightness is an essential criteria for the bridal couple's life attitude. The right bridal bouquet is made with a simple tying technique. A perfect addition: feathers, grasses and long ribbons that flutter playfully in the breeze around the flowers. **(→ p. 16 ff., p. 54 ff., p. 64 f., p. 116 f.)**

4. Sunny-faced flowers are absolutely "in"! Their charming and simple countenances are an expression of harmony and a happy mood par excellence, and therefore virtually tailor-made for bridal floristry. **(→ p. 90 ff.)**

VIEW 2017
Capri

Schmucke BRAUTAUTOS

Für die Fahrt zur Trauung in Standesamt oder Kirche und von dort zum Ort der Feier muss es schon eine besondere, nicht alltägliche Karosse sein. Wirklich individuell und damit absolut einzigartig wird das Brautauto aber erst durch den floralen Schmuck. Wir zeigen Schmuckvarianten rund um einen Oldtimer der 70er Jahre.

WONDERFUL WEDDING CARS. Today's bridal couple needs a special carriage for the drive to the wedding ceremony at the registry office or church and from there to the party venue. But the bridal car only becomes truly unique through its floral decorations. Here we show different designs based on a vintage car from the 1970s.

Die sommerliche Blütenpracht auf dem Heck des Fahrzeugs wird ergänzt um zwei Papeterie-Kreisfächer, die bei der Fahrt fröhlich im Wind tanzen. Das erfordert eine absolut sichere Fixierung.

The beautiful summer flowers on the rear of the car are supplemented by two circular paper rosettes that dance merrily in the wind during the drive. This necessitates an absolutely secure fastening.

FORD
D VIEW 2017

Die gestreckte Girlandenform dieses doppelten Motorhaubenschmucks bezieht sich auf das schnittige Karosseriedesign mit Zierprofilen und Chromstoßstangen.

The elongated garland form of this double hood ornament refers to the streamlined body design with its ornamental strips and chrome bumpers.

VIEW 2017

Die Halbkugeln dieses Dreifachschmucks greifen die üppig gewölbte Blütenform der dominierenden Pfingstrosen auf. Florale Ringe mit Päonienblüten zieren die Türgriffe passend.

The dome shape of this triple adornment emphasizes the ample roundness of the dominating peonies. Matching floral rings with peonies decorate the door handles.

Auf der Fahrt ins Glück sichtet das Brautpaar auf ganzer Breite ein Meer von Blüten voraus, Sinnbild für eine blühende Zukunft.

On their journey to bliss the bridal couple look past a full-width sea of flowers, symbolizing their burgeoning future.

VIEW 2017

Statt über einen Teppich aus Streublumen ins Glück zu schreiten, wird das Brautpaar auf der Fahrt zur Trauung von einem Blütenteppich als Brautautoschmuck begleitet.

Rather than walking down a carpet of strewn flowers on their path to happiness, the bridal couple is escorted to the wedding in a bridal car with a floral carpet on the front.

FORD
D
VIEW 2017

HOCHZEIT IN PASTELL

Passend zur Jahreszeit bestimmt die Leichtigkeit der Blüten in zarten Pastelltönen den Hochzeitsschmuck vom Brautstrauß bis zum Büfett im Freien.

PASTEL WEDDING. Fitting for the season, the lightness of the flowers defines the wedding decorations, from the bridal bouquet to the outdoor buffet.

SWEETEST
thing

Tanja
Simon
Bella

Große Spindelformen mit wehendem Band an hohen Stäben ergänzen im freien Gartenraum als Floralschmuck die Büfettgestecke.

Floral decorations on large spindles, fastened with fluttering ribbons to tall poles standing in the garden, match the buffet table arrangements.

Herzförmige *Dicentra*-Blüten wetteifern im links zu sehenden Brautstrauß mit den Rosen um ihre Bedeutung als Liebessymbol. Der auf dieser Seite gezeigte runde Brautstrauß in etwas kräftigerer Farbgestaltung ist auch als Brautjungfernstrauß geeignet.

In the bridal bouquet on the left, heart-shaped *Dicentra* flowers compete with the roses as symbols of love. The round posy on this page, with a more vibrant colour scheme, is also suitable as a bridesmaid's bouquet.

Maiglöckchen bzw. feine, bewegt schwingende Bänder unterstreichen, passend zum Brautkleid, die zarte und lebensfroh-leichte Ausstrahlung der Brautsträuße.

Matching the bridal gown, lilies of the valley or fine, trailing ribbons emphasize the delicate and carefree charm of the bridal bouquets.

Zauberhaft, wie einem Märchen aus der Zauberwelt der Feen und Wassernixen entsprungen, strahlt die Braut mit ihrem Kopfschmuck und dem passenden Brautstrauß mit abfließenden Bändern.

As if sprung from a tale of fairies and water nymphs, the bride beams enchantingly with her headdress and matching bridal bouquet with cascading ribbons.

At the Riverside

Das Hochzeitfeiern im Freien liegt nach wie vor im Trend. Dabei darf es gerne ein ungewöhnlicher Ort mit besonderer Ausstrahlung sein. Darauf muss auch der Floralschmuck abgestimmt sein, hier in Himmel- und Wasserblau mit Wolkenweiß.

AT THE RIVERSIDE. Open-air wedding celebrations are always en vogue. Especially popular are unusual locations with a special atmosphere. The floral decorations must also match, here in sky and sea blue combined with cumulus white.

Aus den Blütenarten des Brautschmucks ist auch der Floralschmuck der Hochzeitstorte gestaltet, deren Marzipanumhüllung ebenfalls dem grundlegenden Farbkonzept der Hochzeit folgt.

The wedding cake is designed with the same flowers as in the bridal decorations, with a marzipan icing that is also kept in the basic colour scheme of the wedding.

Dieser Brautstrauß zeigt mit der umgekehrten Form eines Tropfens das vom Umfeld vorgegebene Thema „Wasser“. Wellenförmig wird er von Tillandsienblättern durchzogen. Blauer Rittersporn greift in Form von Streublüten am Wasserrand des Flussufers die Farbgestaltung auf.

This bridal bouquet in the shape of an upside-down teardrop reflects the “water” theme dictated by the location. *Tillandsia* leaves are interwoven in a wavelike pattern. Blue larkspur flowers strewn along the water’s edge of the riverbank pick up the colour scheme.

Dieser ebenfalls tropfenförmige Brautstrauß erscheint mit seiner weniger dicht geschlossenen Silhouette und dem Blütenmix verspielter und lockerer. Das symbolische Herz als Strandschmuck wirkt dagegen besonders gut, wenn die Form konkret hervortritt und gleiche Blüten dicht an dicht liegen.

This bridal bouquet also has a teardrop shape, yet appears more playful and light due to its loose silhouette and mix of flowers. The beach decoration in a symbolic heart shape, on the other hand, has maximum impact when flowers of the same variety are closely arranged side by side.

Hochzeit im Vintage-Style

Ein Gewächshaus, das an Pflanzensammlungen des ausgehenden 19. Jahrhunderts erinnert, ist das passende Ambiente für Hochzeiten, bei denen sich eine wundervolle Metamorphose vollzieht: Aus Frauen in ihrer Alltagserscheinung werden strahlend schöne Bräute mit einer Ausstattung im Vintage-Style vom Brautkleid bis zum Blütenschmuck.

VINTAGE WEDDING. A plant collection reminiscent of a conservatory in the late 19th century provides the right atmosphere for weddings. Here a wonderful metamorphosis is taking place: Women in their everyday looks are transformed into radiantly beautiful brides in complete vintage style, from the bridal gowns to the floral decorations.

Der Verzicht auf moderne technische Hilfsmittel bei der Erstellung des Brautstraußes ist im Vintage-Style nur konsequent. Stattdessen passt die ungezwungen wirkende Bündelform in Straußbindetechnik.

Obviously no modern technical aides are necessary for making a bridal bouquet in vintage style. Instead a casual-looking bunch of flowers is created with a simple bouquet-tying technique.

Dieser Brautstrauß zeigt, dass die Bündelform mit parallel zueinander geführten Blütenstielen eine harmonisch gewölbte Kuppelform ohne gequetschte Blüten nicht ausschließt. Im Tischschmuck verweisen einlaminierte Fotodrucke alter botanischer Zeichnungen auf das Gewächshausumfeld.

This bridal bouquet shows how a bunch of flowers with parallel aligned stems can still create a harmonious posy shape without crushing the blooms. The table decorations integrate laminated prints of old botanical drawings as a reference to the conservatory environment.

Dieser Brautstrauß scheint aus Rosen zu bestehen, die soeben im Garten vor dem Gewächshaus gepflückt wurden. Neben der Farbgestaltung dienen vor allem die prachtvoll gefüllten und weit geöffneten Gartenrosenblüten dem stilistischen Ausdruck.

This bridal bouquet is full of roses that appear to have just been picked from the garden outside the greenhouse. In addition to the colour scheme, the style theme is expressed especially well by the luxuriant opulence of double garden roses in full bloom.

Das Integrieren graublättriger Sukkulentenrosetten in den Brautstrauß steht in unmittelbarem Bezug zum Gewächshaus, in dem Hochzeit gefeiert wird. Die sich ergebende leicht morbide Farbwirkung unterstreicht die Vintage-Ausstrahlung.

Integrating greyish-leaved succulents in the bridal bouquet makes a direct reference to the greenhouse where the wedding is being celebrated. The slightly morbid colour effect also emphasizes the vintage charm.

Edle Schlichtheit der Form einerseits, farbliche Abstimmung der dominierenden Blüten auf das Haar der Braut andererseits sowie eine zeitgemäß aktuelle Farbkombination bedingen die stilistisch harmonische Ausstrahlung des Brautstraußes.

Elegant simplicity of form alongside dominating flowers in shades that match the bride's hair are paired up with contemporary colour combinations to create the harmonious impact of this bridal bouquet.

Heiraten im Allgäu

Für die großen Gefühle werden zunehmend theatralische Kulissen gewünscht. Die authentische Alpenszenerie ist dabei sehr beliebt. Dass hier und dabei alles reibungslos gelingt, dafür sorgt die Hochzeitsplanerin Tina Fontana.

ALPINE WEDDING. Demand is increasing for theatrical settings for the big day full of emotions. Authentic alpine scenery is a very popular choice for this. Wedding planner Tina Fontana is always on the spot to make sure everything runs smoothly.

Stilsicher und kreativ gestaltet Tina Fontana Traumhochzeiten vor beeindruckender Bergkulisse im Allgäu. Dabei kann sie nicht nur mit perfekten Kenntnissen der idyllischen Umgebung und Kontakten zu führenden Dienstleistern der Region punkten, sondern macht jedes Event mit ihrer Leidenschaft und Erfahrung, ihrer Liebe zum Detail und ihrem organisatorischen Geschick zum unvergesslichen Fest.

Das Thema der Hochzeit von Julia und Alexander war „Fall in Love". Sie feierten mit ihren Gästen ein herbstlich angehauchtes Fest in warmen Beerentönen und mit edlen Goldakzenten. Die entsprechende Floristik war von opulenten Formen und einer Fülle an Rottönen bestimmt, farblich darauf abgestimmt auch die Papeterie und die liebevoll gestalteten Gastgeschenke. Ein Hauch von frühem Schnee auf den Bergspitzen machte diese Hochzeit zu etwas ganz Besonderem.

Mehr zu und von Tina Fontana:
www.gluecksmomente-allgaeu.de

With creative and confident style, Tina Fontana designs dream weddings with impressive mountain backdrops in the Allgäu region. Not only does she score with perfect knowledge of these idyllic surroundings and her contacts to leading service providers in the area, she also makes every event an unforgettable celebration, thanks to her passion and experience, attention to detail and organizational skills.

The wedding theme for Julia and Alexander was "Fall in Love". Together with their guests, they celebrated the occasion with a hint of autumn. The corresponding floral decorations in warm berry shades and with elegant gold accents was determined by opulent shapes and an array of reds. The paper elements and lovingly designed party favours were also in line with the colour scheme. A hint of early snow on the mountaintops made this wedding even more special.

More about and from Tina Fontana:
www.gluecksmomente-allgaeu.de

Herbstliche Heidehochzeit

In rustikal-ländlichem Stil wird die Heidehochzeit unter freiem Himmel gefeiert. Herbstliche Früchte und Blätter sowie Blüten in entsprechenden Erika-Tönen ergänzen die in allen Floralschmuckelementen dominierende Besenheide.

AUTUMN HEATHER WEDDING. Weddings with Erica are celebrated in the open air with rustic-rural flair. Autumn fruit and leaves as well as flowers in matching hues supplement the common heather that dominates in all floral deco elements.

Wie eine Schar beschwingter Hochzeitsgäste tanzen Dahlienblütenköpfe über einem herbstlich eingefassten Beet aus Heidekraut. Der in Pflanztechnik erstellte Tischschmuck enthält Flaschen, die die Dahlien mit Wasser versorgen.

Like a crowd of jaunty wedding guests, the dahlia flowers bob and sway over a bed of heather framed by autumn florals on the table. The planted centrepiece has bottles inserted to supply the dahlias with water.

Während passend zum Tischschmuck die Serviettenringe aus *Calluna*-Trieben auf Draht gefertigt sind, dienen Strohformen als Basis für die Heidekraut-Herzen, die den Gästen als Willkommensgeschenk überreicht werden.

While the serviette rings are made with *Calluna* shoots wound around wires to match the table decoration, straw bases are used for the heather hearts given to the guests as welcome gifts.

Zu drei farblich voneinander abgesetzten Ringen geformt, umschließt Heidekraut die Blütenkuppel des Brautstraußes und bringt so die hochzeitliche Ringsymbolik in die Gestaltung.

Heather in contrasting colours is fashioned into three rings and added as a collar around the domed bridal bouquet. This brings wedding ring symbolism to the design.

Tütenformen lassen sich aus *Calluna*-Trieben auf Basis von Trockenblumensteckschaum-Kegeln ohne großen Aufwand in Wickeltechnik mithilfe von Zierdraht herstellen. Für den frischen Blütenmix des auf dieser Seite zu sehenden Brautschmucks wird eine Brautstraußsteckbasis eingefügt. Die einfachere, für Brautführerinnen gedachte Tütenfüllung aus Hortensie, mit oder ohne Dahlien, ist mit ein bis zwei Kunststoffwasserröhrchen technisch zu realisieren.

Cones can be shaped effortlessly with *Calluna* shoots based on dry floral foam cones, using a wrapping technique and deco wire. For the bridal bouquet shown on this page mixed fresh flowers are inserted in a foam bouquet holder. The simpler *Hydrangea* cone filling, either with or without dahlias, is meant for the bridesmaids and has one or two plastic water tubes inserted for the flowers.

view

HOCHZEITSGALERIE

Im Folgenden finden Sie eine Vielzahl von Ideen zu thematisch und saisonal unterschiedlich ausgerichteten Hochzeitsfeiern. Ausgewählte Werkstücke zeigen exemplarisch, wie der Style, die Farbgebung oder der Umgang mit den Blumen gedacht ist. Viele der Brautsträuße sind auf Brautstraußhalter gearbeitet, dies hat den Vorteil der schnelleren und damit preisgünstigeren Erstellung. Oder die Brautsträuße sind mit Naturstielen gebunden. Die damit einhergehende natürlich-unkomplizierte Wirkung bräutlichen Floralschmucks liegt nach wie vor im Trend.

Die Werkstoff- und Materiallistungen finden Sie ab Seite 124. Einige der Werkstücke sind mit Preisangaben versehen, die nicht als absolut zu verstehen sind. Die Preise sind nach unseren Einkaufslisten und Arbeitszeiten kalkuliert worden und können regional und saisonal bedingt bis zu 30 % in beide Richtungen abweichen.

ROMANTISCH

VERTRÄUMT

LÄNDLICH

PURISTISCH

NOSTALGISCH

KLASSISCH

EXTRAVAGANT

GALERIE

WEDDING GALLERY

On the following pages you will find a lot of ideas for differently themed wedding celebrations. Select workpieces show examples of our suggestions about style, colour and construction techniques. Many of the bridal bouquets are based on bouquet holders, which not only save time but also offer a cost-effective advantage. Or the bridal bouquets are hand-tied with natural stems. This natural look is still very much en vogue in wedding design at the moment.

You can find the lists of florals and materials on page 124 ff. Some of the workpieces are priced, but these prices are not intended as absolute figures. The prices are calculated according to our procurement lists and worktime and can deviate up to +/- 30 % due to regional and seasonal factors.

Betörender Freesienduft

Der Frühlingswind weht den zarten Duft der Freesien spielerisch über die Hochzeitsfestwiese im Freien.

Passend dazu steht im Hintergrund der Rahmen aus Birkenstämmen und brautweißem Stoff, unter dem sich das Brautpaar das Jawort gibt.

Enchanting freesia scent

A spring breeze playfully wafts the subtle scent of freesias over the meadow wedding venue.

In line with this setting is the frame of birch trunks with draped fabric in wedding white, under which the bride and groom will say their vows.

Wie kleine, dreieckige Wimpel sind die Blütenstände von Freesien geformt. Dennoch lassen sie sich zum kompakten und doch leicht wirkenden Brautstrauß fassen, in dem jede Blüte ihren Platz findet.

The freesia blossoms are shaped like small triangular flags. And yet they can be made into a compact but light bridal bouquet in which every flower is positioned with care

Himmelblaue Perlhyazinthen

Brautstrauß und Tischschmuck werden von Blüten des zeitigen Frühjahrs bestimmt. Deren Zartheit und das vorherrschende Himmelblau der Perlhyazinthen bestimmen eine verträumte, fast mädchenhafte Ausstrahlung.

Für die Leichtigkeit der Anmutung ist es wichtig, dass die Blütenzusammenstellung wirkt, als sei sie auf einem Frühlingsspaziergang frisch gepflückt worden. Technische Akkuratesse der Verarbeitung bleibt dabei dennoch unverzichtbar.

Sky-blue grape

The bridal bouquet and table decorations are dominated by early spring flowers. Their delicate nature and the predominant sky-blue of the grape hyacinths create a dreamy, almost girlish look.

To create the feeling of lightness, it is important for the flower arrangements to appear as if freshly plucked on a spring walk. An accurate floristry technique is nonetheless indispensable.

MR MRS

Trauung mit Tulpen

Tulpen sind mit ihrer runden Blütenform und relativ biegsamen Stielen regelrechte Alleskönner. Der kompakte Bündelbrautstrauß ist damit ebenso möglich, wie der umseitig zu sehende, ausschwingende Armbrautstraußes.

Die gezeigten Brautschmuckkreationen lassen sich in einem einheitlichen Blütenkonzept nutzen. Dann wird der Armbrautstrauß durch die kompakten Brautjungfernsträuße ergänzt oder die kleinere Variante wird zum standesamtlichen Termin gewählt, während der Armstrauß bei der kirchlichen Trauung schmückt.

Tulip wedding

With their rounded flower shape and relatively flexible stems, tulips are true allrounders. In a compact bunch, they are perfect for making a bridal bouquet or the curved bridal arm bouquet illustrated on the next page.

The bridal bouquet creations shown here can be used in a uniform flower concept. The bridal arm bouquet is supplemented by compact bridesmaids' bouquets. Similarly, the smaller version is selected for a civil wedding while the arm bouquet is carried at the church wedding.

Sogenannte Armbrautsträuße werden von der Braut schräg vor dem Körper in der Armbeuge getragen. Dies hat im vorliegenden Fall den Vorteil, dass die bei Tulpen nicht immer vollkommen trockenen Schnittstellen der Stiele nicht unmittelbar das Brautkleid berühren.

The so-called arm bouquet is carried diagonally in front of the bride on her forearm. This has the advantage that any cut tulip stems that are not quite dry will not come in direct contact with the wedding dress.

g&v
GESTALTEN UND VERKAUFEN
GUT ZU WISSEN, WO ICH WEITERE FLORISTIKTRENDS FINDE.
Das ist unser Tag
florist

FRÜHLINGSBUNT zur grünen Hochzeit

Die Initialen der Brautleute, verbunden durch die symbolische Herzform, schmücken die Hochzeitslocation. Das rustikale Astwerk, aus dem diese Buchstaben gefertigt sind, vermittelt den Charme des Selbstgemachten.

Der Herzform liegt eine Frischblumensteckschaum-Basis zugrunde, die die Blüten mit Wasser versorgt. Die Astbuchstaben werden von Zwiebelblumen akzentuiert, die keine zusätzliche Wasserversorgung erfordern.

Spring colours for a green wedding

The initials of the bridal couple, joined by the symbolic heart shape, decorate the wedding venue. The rustic branches with which the letters are formed add homemade charm.

The heart is based on floral foam which supplies the flowers with water. The letters made of branches are accentuated by flowers with bulbs, which don't need any water.

Verführerische Duftnarzissen

Die puristische, modern anmutende Ausstrahlung dieses Brautstraußes wird durch eine einheitliche, lediglich farblich variierte Blütenwahl, die kompakte Bündelform und den haltenden Blätterkragen erzielt.

Um das Spiel der Texturen zwischen den seidigen Blüten und dem Blätterkragen besonders attraktiv zu gestalten, sind die Steineichenblätter so verarbeitet, dass sie ihre wildledern bis samtig erscheinende Unterseite zeigen.

Enticingly fragrant daffodils

The purist and modern look of this bridal bouquet is achieved through a choice of uniform flowers which only vary in colour, the compact posy form and the supporting collar of leaves.

To make the interplay of textures between the silky blossoms and leafy collar particularly appealing, the evergreen oak leaves are applied with their suede and velvety undersides showing.

Wie ein weicher Weg überzieht ein Band aus feinen Flechten den Tisch. Darin eingebettet und von Glasglocken geschützt sind Gruppen zarter Narzissen, wie sie sich auch im Brautstrauß finden.

A strip of fine lichen traverses the table like a fluffy path. Embedded and protected under glass bells are groups of delicate daffodils, matching the flowers in the bridal bouquet.

Jugendlicher Wickencharme

Die pastellene Farbwahl und die seidige Feinheit der Wickenblüten, gepaart mit Häkelspitzen und Etageren in traditioneller Sammeltassen-Optik bewirken das nostalgische Flair dieses Tischschmucks.

Trotz der Reminiszenzen an die Vergangenheit strahlen die Wicken, zwischen die hier und da Rosen gesetzt sind, eine jugendliche Frische aus.

Youthful sweet pea charm

The nostalgic flair of this table decoration comes from the pastel shades and silky delicacy of the sweet pea blossoms, paired with crocheted lace and étagères with traditional collector teacups.

Despite the old-fashioned design, the sweet peas – here and there interspersed with roses – radiate youthful freshness.

Passend zum Stil des Tischschmucks ist der Brautstrauß in traditioneller Tropfenform gestaltet.

In keeping with the style of the table decoration the bridal bouquet is made in the traditional teardrop shape.

BRÄUTLICHE *Bouvardien*

Die klassisch wirkende Strenge der formbinderisch dichten Kugelbasis aus Nelkenblüten wird durch die abfließende, filigrane Kaskade aus Bouvardienblüten und Ranken kontrastiert und spielerisch aufgelöst.

Einzelne Bouvardienblüten sind mithilfe von dünnem Zierdraht aufgefädelt und in den Brautstrauß integriert. Zugleich verleiht der Zierdraht durch Verflechtung mit den Ranken der gesamten Kaskade ihre Form.

Bridal Bouvardia

The classic strictness of the densely-packed circle of carnations in topiary style stands in playful contrast to the cascade of delicate *Bouvardia* flowers and vines flowing down from it.

Single *Bouvardia* blooms are pinned on thin wires and integrated in the bridal bouquet. At the same time, the decorative wire is interwoven with the vines to give the entire cascade its flowing shape.

Eine dicht gefügte Oberfläche aus Blüten zeigt auch der Tischschmuck. Damit für die Gedecke und die tafelnden Gäste genug Platz bleibt, überspielen nur wenige, kurze *Rhipsalis*-Ranken das zentrale Gesteck.

The table decoration also displays a densely-packed silhouette of flowers. To ensure that there is enough room left for the table settings and the guests, only a few short *Rhipsalis* vines flow down from the centrepiece.

Symbolhafte florale Ringe

Ringe symbolisieren die Verbindung, die die Brautleute bei der Trauung eingehen. Diese Symbolik wohnt auch dem aus vier miteinander verbundenen Ringen bestehenden Schmuck für die Hand der Braut inne.

Der Floralschmuck ist formal und stilistisch auf die Erscheinung der Braut abgestimmt. Am deutlichsten wird dies beim gefochtenen Haarkranz als Teil der Frisur.

Symbolic floral rings

Rings are a symbol of unity and a token of the marriage vows taken by the bride and groom. This symbolism is also present in the hand bouquet for the bride, made of four joined floral rings.

In terms of form and design, the floral decorations are tailored to the style of the bride, for example as clearly shown by the braided crown in the bride's coiffure.

Prunkende *Blütenherzen*

Jeweils eine Blütenart in nur einer Farbe bei jeder der Herzformen macht die klassische Ausstrahlung der Reihung aus, die den Weg zur Traukapelle schmückt.

Die Herzen werden von Stäben in Betonwürfeln auf Augenhöhe gehalten. Bräutlich weiße Bänder umwehen sie und lockern den gestalterischen Ausdruck der strengen Reihung auf.

Resplendent floral hearts

Each heart shape is restricted to a single type of flower in the same colour to create the classic flair of this row of sentries guarding the way to the wedding chapel.

The hearts are attached at eye level to poles which are anchored in cement cubes. Ribbons in bridal white flutter around them and loosen up the straight lines of the otherwise strict design.

Das gestalterische Prinzip einer einheitlichen Blütenwahl zeigt auch die aus dicht gefüllten Rosenblüten gesteckte Brautstraußkuppel, die lediglich von einer Nelkenblütenblätterschichtung umschlossen wird.

The design principle of restricting the flowers to a single species is also reflected in the domed bridal bouquet of densely packed roses, which are accompanied only by a collar of white carnation flower petals.

Blütenweiß & Rosenrot

Die romantische Anmutung dieses Brautstraußes basiert auf zwei Faktoren. Zum einen ist dies das feine Spiel zwischen Weißnuancen und rosaroten Tönen, zum anderen die zarte Umkränzung mit rosafarbenem Schleierkraut.

Die Klarheit der Form des A-Linien-Brautkleids und die filigrane Spitze des Oberteils finden in der Brautstraußform und den feinen Schleierkrautblüten ihre Entsprechung.

Lily white and rosy red

The romantic look of this bridal bouquet is based on two factors: the delicate interplay between the shades of white and red on the one hand and the pink *Gypsophila* delicately encircling the arrangement on the other.

The clear A-line of the bridal gown and the filigree lace of the bodice are duplicated in the shape of the bouquet and the fine baby's breath encircling it.

Brautschmuck in Blattmanschette

Naturbezug sowie botanisch inspirierte Formen und Farben liegen im Trend. Vor allem Nuancen von Grün sind unverzichtbar. Tritt Blattwerk im Brautschmuck gleichberechtigt neben die Blüten, ist der trendige Gestaltungsansatz unübersehbar.

Das Blütenbündel im Zentrum dieses trichterförmigen Brautstraußes scheint fast nebensächlich im Vergleich zur Fülle verschiedener Farnblätter, die die Umhüllung bilden.

Bridal designs in leafy collars

The latest trend in wedding design is towards form and colour close to nature or inspired by botanical influences. Nuances of green are a must here. And when the foliage in the bridal bouquet is given as much weight as the flowers, the trendy design concept speaks for itself.

The bunch of flowers in the centre of this funnel-shaped bridal bouquet appears almost insignificant in comparison to the luxuriant mix of ferns forming a collar around the outside.

Die dichte, mehrlagige Manschette aus *Galax*-Blättern, die die Blüten dieses Brautstraußes umgibt, wird mithilfe von Blattwerkkleber auf einem Wellendrahtring gefertigt.

The densely packed layered collar of *Galax* leaves surrounding the flowers in this wedding bouquet is made with the help of foliage glue on a ring of corrugated wire.

Sonnengelbe Hochzeitsreise

Endlich geht's auf Hochzeitsreise und damit auf die Reise ins gemeinsame Leben. Optimistisch strahlendes Gelb und ein nostalgischer Style, der an die 50er Jahre erinnert, begleiten die Braut.

Alte Koffer als Gefäß für den Floralschmuck für die Outdoor-Location und zugleich als Limonaden-Bar passen ebenso perfekt zum nostalgischen Stilkonzept wie die Konzentration auf sonnengesichtige, gelbe Blüten.

Sunny yellow honeymoon

It's finally time for the newlyweds to take off for the honeymoon, commencing their journey into a new life together. Optimistic bright yellow and a nostalgic styling reminiscent of the 1950s accompany the bride.

Antique suitcases hold the floral decorations at the outdoor location and also serve as a lemonade bar, in perfect harmony with the nostalgic design concept and its focus on flowers with sunny yellow faces.

just married

Die bräutlich zarte Ausstrahlung des Brautstraußes wird durch die lockere Anordnung der Blüten und die ausgewogene Mischung zwischen winzigen *Alchemilla*-Blüten und dominierenden Körbchen-Blüten erzielt.

The gentle aura of the bridal bouquet is achieved by the loose arrangement of the flowers and the well-balanced mix of tiny *Alchemilla* blooms and dominating composite flowers from the sunflower family.

Rosencharme *in Pastell*

Vielfarbig pastellene Rosenblüten in Kombination mit Schleiertüll und Schleierblättern vermitteln eine träumerische, fast schwerelose Leichtigkeit in der gestalterischen Wirkung.

Braut-Pomander, kuppelförmiges Tischgesteck und Brautführerinnen- bzw. Standesamtsstrauß folgen demselben gestalterisch-stilistischen Konzept, in dem selbst diese kompakten Formen leicht wirken.

Rose charm in pastels

Roses in different pastel shades in combination with gauzy lace and skeleton leaves transport a dreamy, almost weightless airiness in the design.

The bridal pomander, the dome-shaped table decoration and bouquets for the bridesmaids or registry office follow the same design concept. Even these compact forms have a light and airy appearance.

Die durchschimmernde Stofflichkeit von Tüll bzw. Schleierblättern weisen auch trockene *Lunaria*-Silberlinge auf, die in diesen Straußvarianten verarbeitet sind. Passend dazu die Tüte für die Streublütenblätter.

The transparent gauzy effect of the tulle and the skeleton leaves is also picked up by the dried *Lunaria* medallions integrated in these bouquet variants. A fitting accessory is the cone for the flower girl.

Kombination von Blütenkuppeln

Apricotfarbene Blüten setzen Akzente in diesem ansonsten ganz in Grün und Grüngelb gehaltenen Tischschmuck. Puristisch auch die Beschränkung auf florale Kuppelformen, die über dem Tisch von Papierwabenkugeln aufgegriffen werden.

Ein zusätzlicher Vorteil dieser monoblütigen, hier in langgestreckter Gruppierung verwendeten Tischschmuckelemente ist die modulartig flexible Kombinierbarkeit.

Combination of floral domes

Apricot-coloured flowers add highlights in this otherwise green and yellowish-green table decoration. Add to that the purist reduction to floral domes, a shape that is also reflected in the paper honeycomb balls hanging above the table.

Another advantage of such table elements made with mono flowers, shown here in a long row, is their flexibility for modular combining.

Kuppelform zeigt auch der ganz aus Gladiolenblüten gefertigte Standesamts- bzw. Brautführerinnenstrauß. Für die große Trauzeremonie darf der Brautstrauß üppiger sein und die Form eines umgekehrten Tropfens aufweisen.

The dome shape is also displayed by the bouquet for the bridesmaid or registry office made exclusively of gladiolas. For the main wedding ceremony, the bridal bouquet is allowed to be more luxuriant and fashioned in the shape of an inverted teardrop.

Prunkvoll *gefüllte Lilie*

Klassischer kann man Brautschmuck kaum gestalten, als mit cremeweißen Lilien, die an Wappenlilien alter Zeit erinnern.

Die Glamelie wirkt luxuriös, stellt sie doch eine aus einzelnen Blütenblättern zusammengefügte, üppig vergrößerte Blüte dar. Im Tischschmuck dagegen sind gefüllte Lilienblüten verarbeitet. Da hierbei die Staubblätter in blütenblattähnliche Strukturen umgebildet sind, müssen keine Staubgefäße mehr entfernt werden, die bei normalen Lilien oft zu Verschmutzungen führen.

Magnificent double lilies

Bridal floristry can hardly be more classic than with creamy white lilies, which are reminiscent of heraldic fleur-de-lis on medieval shields.

The glamelia has a luxurious look; it is made of numerous individual flower petals put together in an opulent oversized composite. In the table decoration, however, double lilies are used. As the stamens of these flowers develop into structures similar to flower petals, there is no longer the problem of pollen causing stains, as is often the case with normal lilies.

Rote Dahlien

Nicht immer müssen es Rosen sein, die die Farbe der Liebe mit ihrer erotisch-feurigen Ausstrahlung tragen. In einer in ländlichem Stil gestalteten Brautfloristik übernimmt die Dahlie überzeugend diese Rolle.

Die Dahlien in diesem Brautstrauß werden farblich passend von rotem Laub, rotrindigen Ranken und rötlichen Haselnussfruchtständen begleitet.

Dahlias in fiery red

It doesn't always have to be roses that symbolize the colour of love with their erotic-fiery radiance. Dahlias play the role just as convincingly in this bridal bouquet in a country style.

The dahlias in this bridal bouquet are accompanied by a colour symphony of red: in the leaves, the bark of the vines and the hazelnut infructescence.

Während Ringkissen und Haarschmuck der Braut Dahlie pur zeigen, weist der Floralschmuck für den Bräutigam eine Werkstoffvielfalt wie im Brautstrauß auf, wiederum mit dominierender Dahlie.

While the ring pillow and hair decoration of the bride are made solely with dahlias, the groom's boutonniere displays the same diversity of florals as the bridal bouquet, again with dahlias dominating.

Herbst-Sonne

Diese herbstliche Hochzeitsfloristik vereint, vom Schmuck für die Location im Freien bis zum Brautstrauß mit symbolischem Strohherz, ländlich Traditionelles mit einer zeitgemäß unkonventionellen Gestaltung.

Stroh und Getreide gehören in einen Hochzeitsschmuck in ländlichem Stil, dazu Blüten, wie sie in bunter Mischung in einem bäuerlichen Staudengarten wachsen.

Wedding in the autumn sun

With everything from the decorations for the outdoor venue to the bridal bouquet with a symbolic straw heart, this autumn wedding floristry unites country traditions and floral design with contemporary unconventional flair.

Straw and grain are a must in wedding floristry with a country theme, as well as flowers in a cheerful mix reminiscent of a flower garden on a farm.

Kornähren, Getreidestroh, Äpfel, Hagebutten und Beeren, Sonnenblumen im Brautstrauß und als Ringkissen sowie der Kopfkranz mit Hopfenblütenständen zeigen, dass diese Hochzeit auf dem Lande zur Erntedankzeit gefeiert wird.

Ears of wheat, straw, apples, rose hips, berries and sunflowers in the bridal bouquet and in the ring pillow, together with the hops inflorescence in the flower crown, are proof that this country wedding is being celebrated at Thanksgiving.

Hochzeit zur Hagebuttenzeit

Zwischen der Ausstrahlung eines üppig-ländlichen Erntedankfests und puristischer Beschränkung in der floralen Gestaltung entwickelt dieser Brautschmuck eine modern wirkende und doch nostalgische Anmutung.

Von der Hagebutte als farbbestimmendem Werkstoff über das gerundete Ringkissen bis zum Brautstrauß in Kugelform beherrscht ein durchgängiges Formprinzip die Gestaltung.

Wedding in rose hip season

Between the ambience of a bountiful Thanksgiving celebration in the country and the floral design in a purist style, this bridal bouquet creates a modern yet nostalgic atmosphere.

From the rose hips in charge of the colour scheme to the round ring pillow and the bridal bouquet in the shape of a ball, all elements of the design follow the same form principle.

Guten Hunger!

Die farbliche Pracht von Hagebutten, ergänzt um das Orange der ungleich größeren Kürbisse, bestimmt auch den Floralschmuck des Getränkebüfetts in der zum ländlich-nostalgischen Stil der Hochzeit passenden Scheune als dem Ort der Feier.

The colour splendour of rose hips goes hand-in-hand with the medley of ornamental squash in orange. Together they set the stage for the floral decorations on the drinks buffet in the wedding hall – a barn that fits in well with the country-nostalgic style of the celebrations.

Südafrikanischer Brautschmuck

Auch in Zeiten weltweiter Vernetzung und einer relativ guten Erreichbarkeit selbst der entferntesten Reiseziele strahlt Hochzeitsschmuck aus exotischen Werkstoffen, die in fernen Ländern beheimatet sind, Extravaganz aus.

Dieser aus sogenannten Kapgrün-Arten und Eukalyptuslaub gestaltete Raumschmuck für ein Hochzeitsfest erinnert an Traumfänger und weist womöglich bereits auf das entsprechend traumhafte Hochzeitsreiseziel hin.

South African wedding design

Even in times of global networking and relatively good connections to even the most remote travel destinations, wedding decorations made with exotic materials from distant lands radiate extravagance.

This room decoration for a wedding celebration, made with proteas and *Eucalyptus* leaves, is reminiscent of dreamcatchers and could be an indication of an equally wonderful honeymoon destination.

Serruria florida, die errötende Braut, wie ihr englischer Name lautet, ist die Blütenschönheit in der Fülle unterschiedlicher botanischer Werkstoffe von der südafrikanischen Kapregion, aus denen dieser Brautstrauß ausschließlich gefertigt ist.

Serruria florida, also known by its English common name "blushing bride", is the beautiful flower amidst a plethora of various botanical materials from the South African Cape region in this reduced bridal bouquet.

Winterblühende Purpur-Lenzrose

So lebensstark robust sie als Winterblüherin sein muss, so zart und edel ist die Wirkung insbesondere der dunklen Purpur-Lenzrose. Diese Eigenschaften ergeben, kombiniert mit einer unkompliziert einfachen Verarbeitung, die romantische Ausstrahlung.

Die kompakte Brautstraußform einerseits und der ungebändigt wirkende Charakter des Büfettschmucks andererseits werden gestalterisch durch die einheitliche Blütenwahl geklammert. Reproduktionen alter Drucke von *Helleborus* unterstreichen das Blütenthema.

Winter blooming hellebores in purple

While winter bloomers must be robust to survive, the look of dark-purple hellebores in particular is every bit as delicate and elegant. These characteristics, combined with a simple floristry technique, result in romantic radiance.

The compact shape of the bridal bouquet on the one hand and the untamed nature of the buffet decoration on the other, are brought together by a uniform choice of flowers. Reproductions of old *Helleborus* prints underscore the flower theme.

Wünsche
werden wahr

Wer würde einem Brautpaar nicht alle erdenklichen Segenswünsche übermitteln wollen? Hier werden sie in Glasfläschchen an einem Wunschbaum gesammelt, der besonders am Abend seine romantische Wirkung durch eine Fülle integrierter Lämpchen entfalten wird.

Geschmückt ist der Wunschbaum mit feingliedrigen Waldrebenfruchtständen, auf die auch die Herzkelchblüten des Brautstraußes gebettet sind.

Dreams come true

Who wouldn't want to convey all the best wishes imaginable to the bridal couple? Here they are collected in small glass bottles hanging from a wish tree, which unfurls its romantic effect especially in the evening with strings of integrated fairy lights.

The wish tree is decorated with fine *Clematis* infructescence, on which the *Eucharis* flowers of the bridal bouquet are also embedded.

Bedeutung der Symbole | abbreviation symbols:

◖5 € ●10 € ▬50 €

H Höhe | height

Ø Durchmesser | diameter

◷ Fertigungszeit für einen geübten Floristen | work time for a practised florist

€ Preisgruppe als Orientierung | price group as orientation

Einige Werkstücke sind mit Preisangaben versehen. Diese können je nach Region oder Saison abweichen und dienen lediglich als Orientierung.

Some of the workpieces have prices. These can vary according to region and season and serve soley for orientation purposes.

6–7

Dahlia Cultivar, Eustoma grandiflorum, Hosta Cultivar, Rosa Cultivar, Scabiosa atropurpurea, Spiraea x arguta

Band | ribbon (Goldina)
Papierkreisfächer | paper rosettes (Wabenball)
Bambusstäbe | bamboo sticks
Stützdraht | stay wire (Buco)
Autoschmuck-Steckbasis mit Saugnapf | car deco foam base with suction cup (Oasis)

8–9

Alchemilla mollis, Limonium tetragonum, Rosa Cultivars, Thlaspi arvense

Furnierstreifen | veneer strips
Kordel | cord
Rebenbindedraht | florists' twine (Buco)
Saugnäpfe | suction cups (Oasis)

10–11

Alchemilla mollis, Eustoma grandiflorum, Geranium macrorrhizum, Nigella damascena, Paeonia lactiflora, Rosa Cultivar

Tüll | tulle
Band | ribbon (Goldina)
Zierdraht | deco wire (Buco)
Stützdraht | stay wire (Buco)
Kunststoffwasserröhrchen | plastic water tubes
Autoschmuck-Steckbasen mit Saugnapf | car deco foam bases with suction cup (Oasis)

12–13

Alchemilla mollis, Antirrhinum majus, Eustoma grandiflorum, Panicum setaceum, Rosa Cultivar, Scabiosa caucasica, Viburnum lantana

Zierdraht | deco wire (Buco)
Saugnäpfe | suction cups (Oasis)
Frischblumensteckschaum-Girlande | floral foam garland (Oasis)

14–15

Antirrhinum majus, Delphinium Cultivar, Hydrangea macrophylla, Nigella damascena, Olea europaea, Pteris cretica, Rosa Cultivar

Band | ribbon (Goldina)
Nesselstoff | muslin
Garn | yarn
Abtönfarbe | paint
Saugnäpfe | suction cups (Oasis)
Floralkleber | floral adhesive (Oasis)

16–17

Dianthus caryophyllus, Dichondra argentea 'Silver Falls', Eustoma grandiflorum, Paeonia lactiflora, Phlox paniculata, Rosa Cultivar, Spiraea x arguta, Apfelbaumzweige | apple branches

Gefäße | containers (Serax)
Drahtgeflecht | wire mesh
Tonkinstäbe | tonkin sticks
Frischblumensteckschaum-Ziegel | floral foam brick (Oasis)

weitere im Bild zu erkennende Produkte:
Teller | plates (ASA)
Gläser | glasses (Zwiesel)
Tabletts | trays (D&M Depot)
Bonbon Gläser | candy jars (Leonardo)
Bowle | punch bowl (Klocke)

18–19

Eustoma grandiflorum, Paeonia lactiflora, Phlox paniculata, Rosa Cultivar, Syringa vulgaris, Thlaspi arvense, Viburnum opulus 'Roseum', Zweige | twigs

Rebenbindedraht | florists' twine (Buco)
Zierdraht | deco wire (Buco)
Band | ribbon (Goldina)
Glasröhrchen | glass tubes
Holzstäbe | wooden sticks
Farbspray | spray paint (Oasis)

20

Dianthus caryophyllus, Dicentra spectabilis, Dichondra argentea 'Silver Falls', Ranunculus Cultivar, Rosa Cultivar, Syringa vulgaris, Viburnum opulus 'Roseum'

Band | ribbon (Goldina)
Heißkleber | hot glue (Oasis)
Brautstraußsteckbasis | bridal bouquet holder (Oasis)

21

Bouvardia Cultivar, Lathyrus odoratus, Paeonia lactiflora, Ranunculus Cultivar, Rosa Cultivar

Band | ribbon (Goldina)
Stützdraht | stay wire (Buco)
Heißkleber | hot glue (Oasis)
Brautstraußsteckbasis | bridal bouquet holder (Oasis)

22

Convallaria majalis, Muehlenbeckia axillaris, Olea europaea, Phlox paniculata, Ranunculus Cultivar, Rosa Cultivar, Stachys byzantina

Band | ribbon (Goldina)
Heißkleber | hot glue (Oasis)
Brautstraußsteckbasis | bridal bouquet holder (Oasis)

23

Bouvardia Cultivar, Dianthus caryophyllus, Lathyrus odoratus, Paeonia lactiflora, Phlebodium aureum, Ranunculus Cultivar, Rosa Cultivar, Stachys byzantina

Band | ribbon (Goldina)
Heißkleber | hot glue (Oasis)
Brautstraußsteckbasis | bridal bouquet holder (Oasis)

SERVICE

LIST OF FLORALS AND MATERIALS

24
Centaurea cyanus, Delphinium Cultivar, Gypsophila paniculata, Stachys byzantina

Perlenringe | beaded rings
Band | ribbon (Goldina)
Zierdraht | deco wire (Buco)
Brautstraußsteckbasis | bridal bouquet holder (Oasis)

25
Delphinium Cultivar, Gypsophila paniculata

Hochzeitstorte | wedding cake (Die Nascherei)
Band | ribbon (Goldina)
Zierdraht | deco wire (Buco)

27
Delphinium Cultivar, Gypsophila paniculata, Hydrangea macrophylla

Band | ribbon (Goldina)
Zierdraht | deco wire (Buco)
Floralkleber | floral adhesive (Oasis)

29
Delphinium Cultivar, Hydrangea macrophylla, Tillandsia xerographica

Band | ribbon (Goldina)
Zierdraht | deco wire (Buco)
Stützdraht | stay wire (Buco)
Floralkleber | floral adhesive (Oasis)
Floraltape | floral tape (Oasis)
Brautstraußsteckbasis | bridal bouquet holder (Oasis)

30
Centaurea cyanus, Clematis Cultivar, Nigella damascena, Ozothamnus diosmifolius, Rosa Cultivar, Ranken | vines

Band | ribbon (Goldina)
Brautstraußsteckbasis | bridal bouquet holder (Oasis)

33
Astilbe x arendsii, Astrantia major, Callistephus chinensis, Eucalyptus cinerea, Eustoma grandiflora, Helichrysum italicum, Rosa Cultivar

Perlenschnur | string of pearls
Band | ribbon (Goldina)
Bindebast | bast

34
Callistephus chinensis, Dianthus caryophyllus, Hydrangea arborescens, Scabiosa atropurpurea, Scabiosa stellata, Sedum telephium

Band | ribbon (Goldina)
Stützdraht | stay wire (Buco)
Bindebast | bast

35
Astilbe x arendsii, Astrantia major, Callistephus chinensis, Eucalyptus cinerea, Rosa Cultivar, Scabiosa stellata, Sedum telephium, Xanthorrhoea australis, Moos | moss

Glasschale | glass bowl
Glasflaschen | glass bottles
Astscheiben | branch slices
Pflanzendrucke | plant prints
Frischblumensteckschaum-Ziegel | floral foam brick (Oasis)

36–37
Astilbe x arendsii, Geranium macrorrhizum, Hydrangea arborescens, Rosa Cultivars

Band | ribbon (Goldina)
Bindebast | bast

38–39
Ceropegia linearis woodii, Echeveria Cultivar, Eustoma grandiflorum, Kalanchoe blossfeldiana, Rosa Cultivars, Scabiosa stellata, Sedum telephium

Band | ribbon (Goldina)
Stützdraht | stay wire (Buco)
Bindebast | bast

40–41
Astilbe x arendsii, Astrantia major, Bouvardia Cultivar, Eucalyptus cinerea, Helichrysum italicum, Rosa Cultivars

Band | ribbon (Goldina)
Bindebast | bast

46–48
Aesculus hippocastanum, Calluna vulgaris, Clematis vitalba, Dahlia Cultivar, Fagus sylvatica, Malus Cultivar, Quercus robur

Holzkisten | wooden crates (Gasper)
Glasflaschen | glass bottles
Wickeldraht | binding wire (Buco)

weitere im Bild zu erkennende Produkte:
Geschirr | dishes (Broste)

49
Calluna vulgaris, Dahlia Cultivar, Rosa Cultivar, Scabiosa atropurpurea, Symphoricarpos x doorenbosii

Band | ribbon (Goldina)
Zierdraht | deco wire (Buco)
Wellendrahtring | corrugated wire ring (Buco)
Bindebast | bast

50–51
Calluna vulgaris, Convolvulus arvensis, Dahlia Cultivar, Hydrangea macrophylla, Ozothamnus diosmifolius, Rosa Cultivar, Scabiosa atropurpurea, Symphoricarpos x doorenbosii

Band | ribbon (Goldina)
Zierdraht | deco wire (Buco)
Kunststoffwasserröhrchen | plastic water tubes
Trockenblumensteckschaum-Kegel | dry floral foam cone (Oasis)

BARENDSEN
FLOWERS·AALSMEER
www.barendsen.nl

GLASS HOUSE TALK

Jan de Boer ist Leiter des Unternehmens Barendsen B.V., das schon über 100 Jahre via Bloemenveiling Aalsmeer/NL im- und exportiert. In dieser Rubrik möchte er für gärtnerische Spezialprodukte Aufmerksamkeit wecken. Hier stellt er die neue ***Rosa 'Alabaster'*** vor.

Welche Rosen sind prädestiniert für die Brautfloristik?
Wir lieben Gartenrosen wegen ihrer spektakulär gefüllten Blüte mit unzähligen Blütenblättern und ihrem wunderbaren Duft. Das sind perfekte Brautblüten! Und unter all den Rosensorten ist es die reinweiße Premium Gartenrose ***'Alabaster'*** von **Parfum Flower Company,** die sich besonders für eine weiße Hochzeit eignet.

Benötigen Gartenrosen eine bestimmte Behandlung?
Gartenrosen unterscheiden sich von Gewächshausware. Mit der richtigen Behandlung schenken sie viel Freude! Wussten Sie z. B., dass diese Rosen mit ihren sogenannten Regenblättern angeliefert werden, die, meist bräunlich, die Blüte schützend umhüllen? Bei Anlieferung sollten daher fünf bis zehn dieser äußeren Blütenblätter entfernt werden.

Spielt die Art der Anlieferung für die Weiterbehandlung eine Rolle?
Ja, es macht einen Unterschied, ob die Rosen trocken oder in Wasser stehend angeliefert werden. Trocken angelieferte Ware wird, noch bevor die Verpackung geöffnet wird, angeschnitten und für einige Stunden in Wasser mit Frischblumennahrung gestellt. Auf diese Weise sollten sie sich im gekühlten Raum vier bis fünf Stunden erholen, ehe sie in den Verkauf gehen. Kommen die Rosen in Wasser stehend an, können sie zum Weiterverkauf unmittelbar ausgepackt, geputzt, angeschnitten und in Wasser mit Blumenfrischhaltemittel eingestellt werden.

Was ist zu beachten, damit die Rosen ihre Wirkung voll entfalten können?
Sind die Rosen für ein Event bestimmt, sollten sie vier bis fünf Tage Zeit bekommen, um sich vollständig zu entwickeln. Die geöffneten Blüten zeigen dann ihre ganze Schönheit und bereichern das Event mit ihrer märchenhaften Ausstrahlung.

Was zeichnet die Sorte *'Alabaster'* insbesondere aus?
'Alabaster' ist eine großblütige und duftende Sorte in Weiß. Ca. 60 Blütenblätter und ein Blütendurchmesser bis sieben Zentimeter verleihen ihr eine beeindruckende Blütenwirkung. Weitere Vorteile: Sie ist ganzjährig verfügbar und hat eine Haltbarkeit von bis zu zehn Tagen!

Jan de Boer is the director of Barendsen B.V., a company that has been im- and exporting plants and flowers via the Aalsmeer flower auction in the Netherlands for over 100 years. In this article, he would like to draw attention to ***Rosa 'Alabaster':***
We just love the garden roses because of their spectacular bloom with layers and layers of petals and the most wonderful fragrance. They are the perfect wedding flower. And among these roses, the pristine white ***'Alabaster'*** from the **Parfum Flower Company** is especially well suited for white weddings! Garden roses however have special needs. Did you know that these roses are shipped with guard petals which turn brown and should be removed on arrival, up to 10 petals per bloom? And there are different ways of handling the flowers when arriving in boxes or in water buckets. When they arrive in boxes you should first cut the stems and hydrate the flowers a few hours (4–5 hours) in water with flower food before removing the packaging. And if they arrive in water buckets you should remove the packaging, cut the stems and put them in water with flower food right away. If you want to use them for an event, give them ample time to open fully. They will be at their most beautiful and will bring that fairytale quality to your event. With 60 petals, a diameter of 6–8 cm, a vase life up to 10 days and a year round availability ***'Alabaster'*** finally is a great white variety with a fragrance for both events and vase work!

WERKSTOFF- UND MATERIALLISTUNG

54–56
Freesia Cultivars, Jasminum polyanthum, Birkenäste, Birkenstämme | birch branches, trunks

Stoffstreifen | strips of fabric
Drahtkäfige | wire cages (Klocke)
Metallstäbe mit Betonwürfeln | metal poles on cement cubes (Freese)
Frischblumensteckschaum-Ziegel | floral foam brick (Oasis)

57
Freesia Cultivars

Band | ribbon (Goldina)
Bindebast | bast

H *22 cm* Ø *23 cm*
⏲ *30 min* €

58
Anemone blanda, Anemone nemorosa, Fritillaria meleagris, Jasminum polyanthum, Muscari armeniacum, Myosotis sylvatica, Ornithogalum umbellatum, Scilla peruviana, Viola cornuta

Band | ribbon (Goldina)
doppelseitiges Transparentklebeband | double-sided clear tape (Oasis)
Brautstraußsteckbasis | bridal bouquet holder (Oasis)

H *26 cm* Ø *15 cm*
⏲ *30 min* €

59
Anemone blanda, Fritillaria meleagris, Jasminum polyanthum, Muscari armeniacum, Salix caprea, Thymus vulgaris, Zweige | twigs

Schnur | string (Goldina)
Schale | bowl (Klocke)
Glasbecher | glasses
Gummiband | rubber band

weitere im Bild zu erkennende Produkte:
Geschirr | dishes (ASA)
Gläser | glasses (Zwiesel)
Fliesen | tiles (Klocke)

60–61
Amelanchier lamarckii, Ranunculus asiaticus, Spiraea x arguta, Stachys byzantina, Tulipa Cultivar

Band | ribbon (Goldina)
Floraltape | floral tape (Oasis)

62
Allium neapolitanum, Aristea confusa, Geranium macrorrhizum, Hosta Cultivar, Jasminum polyanthum, Leucojum vernum, Spiraea x arguta, Tulipa Cultivar

Band | ribbon (Goldina)
Bindebast | bast
Floraltape | floral tape (Oasis)

64
Anemone coronaria, Fritillaria meleagris, Jasminum polyanthum, Limonium tetragonum, Myosotis sylvatica, Ranunculus asiaticus, Tulipa Cultivar, Viola cornuta, Zweige | twigs

Band | ribbon (Goldina)
Zierdraht | deco wire (Buco)
Stützdraht | stay wire (Buco)
Floralkleber | floral adhesive (Oasis)
Brautstraußsteckbasis | bridal bouquet holder (Oasis)

H *20 cm* Ø *21 cm*
⏲ *45 min* €

65
Anemone coronaria, Bellis perennis, Fritillaria meleagris, Jasminum polyanthum, Limonium tetragonum, Muscari armeniacum, Narcissus Cultivar, Ranunculus asiaticus, Tulipa Cultivar, Viburnum opulus 'Roseum', Viola cornuta, Holunderäste | juniper branches, Moos | moss

Efeunadeln | ivy pins (Buco)
Zahnstocher | toothpicks
Schrauben | screws
Heißkleber | hot glue (Oasis)
Frischblumensteckschaum-Herz mit Kunststoffunterlage | floral foam heart with plastic tray (Oasis)

66–67
Narcissus Cultivars, Quercus ilex, Viburnum opulus 'Roseum'

Band | ribbon (Goldina)
Stützdraht | stay wire (Buco)
Kunststoffsteckvase | plastic vase
Bindebast | bast
Floraltape | floral tape (Oasis)
doppelseitiges Transparentklebeband | double-sided clear tape (Oasis)

H *29 cm* Ø *17 cm*
⏲ *45 min* €

68–69
Cladonia rangiferina, Narcissus Cultivars, Zweige | twigs

Glasglocken | glass bell (Klocke)
Zierdraht | deco wire (Buco)
Untersetzer | coasters
Frischblumensteckschaum-Ziegel | floral foam brick (Oasis)

weitere im Bild zu erkennende Produkte:
Geschirr | dishes (ASA)
Gläser | glasses (Zwiesel)

70–71
Dichondra argentea 'Silver Falls', Lathyrus odoratus, Rosa Cultivar, Stachys byzantina

Etageren | étagères (My Etagere)
Glasglocke | glass bell
Frischblumensteckschaum-Ziegel | floral foam brick (Oasis)

72–73
Dichondra argentea 'Silver Falls', Lathyrus odoratus, Rosa Cultivar, Stachys byzantina

Band | ribbon (Goldina)
Brautstraußsteckbasis | bridal bouquet holder (Oasis)

L *46 cm* Ø *28 cm*
⏲ *25 min* €

74–75
Bouvardia Cultivar, Ceropegia linearis subsp. woodii, Dianthus caryophyllus, Rhipsalis capilliformis

Band | ribbon (Goldina)
Zierdraht | deco wire (Buco)
Brautstraußsteckbasis | bridal bouquet holder (Oasis)

L *60 cm* Ø *20 cm*
⏲ *45 min* €

76–77
Bouvardia Cultivar, Ceropegia linearis subsp. woodii, Dianthus caryophyllus, Rhipsalis capilliformis, Rosa Cultivar

Kerzen | candles
Kerzenhalter | candle holder
Kunststoffschale mit Frischblumensteckschaum | plastic tray with floral foam (Oasis)

weitere im Bild zu erkennende Produkte:
Geschirr | dishes (ASA)
Gläser | glasses (Zwiesel)
Stühle | chairs (KFF)

78–79
Ajania pacifica, Alchemilla mollis, Helipterum manglesii, Lavandula angustifolia, Rosa Cultivar

Band, Zierdraht | ribbon, deco wire (Buco)
Floraltape | floral tape (Oasis)
Wellendrahtringe | corrugated wire rings (Buco)

80 & 82
Dianthus caryophyllus, Rosa Cultivar

Band | ribbon (Goldina)
Stützdraht | stay wire (Buco)
Kunststoffhalbkugel | plastic semi-sphere
Floralkleber | floral adhesive (Oasis)
Brautstraußsteckbasis | bridal bouquet holder (Oasis)

H *21 cm* Ø *20 cm*
⏲ *30 min* €

81 & 83
Dianthus caryophyllus, Eustoma grandiflorum, Gypsophila paniculata, Rosa Cultivar

Band | ribbon (Goldina)
Stützdraht | stay wire (Buco)
Metallstäbe mit Betonwürfel | metal poles with cement cubes (Freese)
Frischblumensteckschaum-Herzen auf Holzbasis | floral foam hearts on wooden base (Oasis)

84–85
Alchemilla mollis, Eustoma grandiflorum, Gypsophila paniculata, Nigella damascena, Rosa Cultivars

Band | ribbon
Bindebast | bast
Corsagenclip | corsage clip (Oasis)

86–87
Akebia quinata, Asplenium antiquum, Nephrolepis exaltata, Rosa Cultivars, Sticherus flabellatus, Zinnia elegans

Band | ribbon (Goldina)
Bindebast | bast
Floraltape | floral tape (Oasis)

88–89
Dicentra spectabilis, Rosa Cultivar, Zinnia elegans

Band | ribbon (Goldina)
Wellendrahtring | corrugated wire ring (Buco)
Stützdraht | stay wire (Buco)
Bindebast | bast
Floralkleber | floral adhesive (Oasis)
Tape | tape (Oasis)

H *25 cm* Ø *22 cm*
⏲ *30 min* €

91
Alchemilla mollis, Argyranthemum frutescens, Gypsophila paniculata, Lantana camara

Band | ribbon (Goldina)
Papierkreisfächer | paper rosettes (Wabenball)
alte Koffer | antique suitcases
Tapete | wallpaper
Wickeldraht | binding wire (Buco)
Folie | foil
Kordel | cord
Kaltkleber | cold adhesive
Getränkeflaschen | bottles
Tische | tables

92–93
Alchemilla mollis, Aquilegia caerulea, Argyranthemum frutescens, Bidens ferulifolia, Rosa Cultivar, Zinnia Cultivars

Band | ribbon (Goldina)
Bindebast | bast

H *27 cm* Ø *25 cm*
⏲ *30 min* €

94
Lunaria annua, Rosa Cultivar

Band | ribbon (Goldina)
Tüll | tulle
Steckdraht | support wire (Buco)
Ziernadeln | deco pins (Oasis)
Frischblumensteckschaum-Kugel im Netz | netted floral foam sphere (Oasis)

Ø *20 cm*
⏲ *35 min* €

95 oben | above
Rosa Cultivar

Maulbeerrindenfasern | mulberry bark fibre
Tüll | tulle
Bindebast | bast
Stützdraht | stay wire (Buco)
Zierstecknadeln | deco pins (Oasis)

H *26 cm* Ø *25 cm*
30 min €

95 unten | below
Rosa Cultivar

Schleierblätter | skeleton leaves
Schale | bowl (D&M Depot)
Zierstecknadeln | deco pins (Oasis)
Frischblumensteckschaum-Kugel | floral foam sphere (Oasis)

96
Lunaria annua, Rosa Cultivar, Schleierblätter | skeleton leaves

Band | ribbon (Goldina)
Tüll | tulle
Perlen | beads
Papier | paper
Steckdraht | support wire (Buco)
Bast | bast

97
Achillea millefolium, Dianthus caryophyllus, Lunaria annua, Rosa Cultivar, Trifolium ochroleucum, Schleierblätter | skeleton leaves

Ziernadeln | deco pins
Bindebast | bast
Stützdraht | stay wire (Buco)

H *30 cm* Ø *27 cm*
30 min €

98–99
Brassica napus, Dianthus barbatus, Dianthus caryophyllus, Eustoma grandiflorum, Gerbera jamesonii, Triticum aestivum

Gefäße | containers (Dutz)
Papierwabenbälle | paper honeycomb balls
Bindebast | bast

weitere im Bild erkennbare Elemente:
Geschirr | dishes (ASA)
Gläser | glasses (Zwiesel)
Kerzen | candles (Wenzel)
Servietten | serviettes (Kardelen)

100
Anethum graveolens, Dianthus caryophyllus, Lewisia cotyledon, Muehlenbeckia axillaris, Rosa Cultivar, Zinnia elegans

Band | ribbon (Goldina)
Heißkleber | hot glue (Oasis)
Brautstraußsteckbasis | bridal bouquet holder (Oasis)

101
Gladiole Cultivar

Band | ribbon (Goldina)
Pappkartonkreisscheibe | cardboard disk
Brautstraußsteckbasis | bridal bouquet holder (Oasis)

102
Lilium orientale 'Roselily Carolina', Stachys byzantina

Band | ribbon (Goldina)
Zierdraht | deco wire (Buco)
Myrtendraht | myrtle wire (Buco)
Floraltape | floral tape (Oasis)

H *21 cm* Ø *25 cm*
100 min €

103
Geranium macrorrhizum, Hydrangea arborescens, Lilium orientale 'Roselily Carolina', Rosa Cultivars

Frischblumensteckschaum-Kranz mit Hartschaumunterlage | floral foam wreath with hard foam tray (Oasis)

weitere im Bild zu erkennende Produkte:
Geschirr | dishes (ASA)
Gläser | glasses (Zwiesel)
Kerzen | candles (Wenzel)

H *20 cm* Ø *45 cm*
20 min €

104–105
Akebia quinata, Alstroemeria Cultivar, Corylus avellana, Cotinus coggygria, Dahlia Cultivar, Heuchera Cultivar, Rosa Cultivar

Band | ribbon (Goldina)
Brautstraußsteckbasis | bridal bouquet holder (Oasis)

H *25 cm* Ø *28 cm*
25 min €

106
Akebia quinata, Dahlia Cultivar

Körbchen | basket
Folie | foil
Frischblumensteckschaum-Ziegel | floral foam brick (Oasis)

107
Alstroemeria Cultivar, Corylus avellana, Dahlia Cultivar, Heuchera Cultivar, Rosa Cultivar

Myrtendraht | myrtle wire (Buco)
Corsageclip | corsage clip (Oasis)
Floralkleber | floral adhesive (Oasis)

108–109
Aster novi-belgii, Chasmanthium latifolium, Craspedia globosa, Dahlia Cultivar, Daucus carota, Helianthus annuus, Humulus lupulus, Rudbeckia hirta, Viburnum opulus, Stroh | straw, Äste | branches

Band | ribbon (Goldina)
Drahtkorb | wire basket (Dijk)
Zierdraht | deco wire (Buco)
Steckdraht | support wire (Buco)
Schrauben | screws
Kunststoffschale mit Frischblumensteckschaum | plastic tray with floral foam (Oasis)

110
Humulus lupulus, Hydrangea macrophylla, Rosa virginiana

Zierdraht | deco wire (Buco)

111
Aster novi-belgii, Craspedia globosa, Helenium Cultivar, Helianthus annuus, Malus Cultivars, Symphoricarpos x doorenbosii, Zinnia elegans, Stroh | straw

Band | ribbon (Goldina)
Zierdraht | deco wire (Buco)
Stützdraht | stay wire (Buco)
Pappkartonkreisscheibe | cardboard disk
Floraltape | floral tape (Oasis)

H *25 cm* Ø *20 cm*
40 min €

112
Craspedia globosa, Echinacea purpurea, Malus Cultivar, Rubus 'Thornless Evergreen', Hagebutten | rose hips

Band | ribbon (Goldina)
Stützdraht | stay wire (Buco)
Bindebast | bast
Floraltape | floral tape (Oasis)

H *28 cm* Ø *20 cm*
30 min €

113 oben | above
Hagebutten | rose hips

Holzscheibe | wooden disk
Zahnstocher | toothpicks
Trockenblumensteckschaum-Halbkugel | dry floral foam semi-sphere (Oasis)

116–117
Berzelia lanuginosa, Brunia laevis, Eucalyptus polyanthemos, Leucadendron galpinii, Lunaria annua, Ozothamnus diosmifolius, Protea Cultivar, Serruria florida

Wolle | wool (Lehner)
Band | ribbon (Goldina)
Leinenstoff | linen
Zierdraht | deco wire (Buco)
Drahtring | wire ring (Buco)

118–119
Berzelia lanuginosa, Brunia laevis, Leucadendron galpinii, Ozothamnus diosmifolius, Phylica lasiocarpa, Protea Cultivar, Serruria florida

Band | ribbon (Goldina)
Brautstraußsteckbasis | bridal bouquet holder (Oasis)

H *23 cm* Ø *25 cm*
15 min €

120
Eucalyptus polyanthemos, Helleborus Cultivars, Ranunculus asiaticus

Band | ribbon (Goldina)
Wellendrahtring | corrugated wire ring (Buco)
Bindebast | bast
Floraltape | floral tape (Oasis)
Floralkleber | floral adhesive (Oasis)

H *26 cm* Ø *22 cm*
60 min €

121
Fritillaria meleagris, Hedera helix, Helleborus Cultivars, Narcissus Cultivar, Ranunculus asiaticus, Spiraea x arguta, Zweige | twigs

Glasgefäße | glass containers
Pflanzendrucke | plant prints
Bindebast | bast

weitere im Bild zu erkennende Produkte:
Windlicht | hurricane lamp (Serax)
Koffer | suitcase (Dijk)

122
Clematis vitalba, Lunaria annua, verzweigter Ast | branch

Band | ribbon (Goldina)
Glasfläschchen | small glass bottles
Schmuckornamente | ornaments
Flaschen-Lichterkette | bottle fairy lights
Architektenpapier | drafting paper
Betonfuß | cement foot
Farbspray | spray paint (Oasis)
Heißkleber | hot glue (Oasis)

weitere im Bild zu erkennende Produkte:
Vase | vase (Fink)
Sektkühler | champagne cooler (Fink)
Tisch | table (Fink)
Gläser | glasses (Zwiesel)

123
Clematis vitalba, Dianthus caryophyllus, Eucharis x grandiflora, Eustoma grandiflorum, Rosa Cultivar, Ranken | vines

Band | ribbon (Goldina)
Brautstraußsteckbasis mit Metallic-Griff | bridal bouquet holder with metal handle (Oasis)

H *30 cm* Ø *25 cm*
35 min €

Herausgeber 🌐 Publisher
Bezugsadresse 🌐 Source
BLOOM's GmbH
Am Potekamp 6
40885 Ratingen (D)
T +49 2102 9644-0
F +49 2102 896073
info@blooms.de
www.blooms.de

Geschäftsführung 🌐 Management
Andrea Rothe
Klaus Wagener

Anzeigen 🌐 Advertising
Nina Schulz

Chefredaktion 🌐 Editor in Chief
Hella Henckel

Redaktion 🌐 Technical Editor
Karl-Michael Haake

Floristische Konzeption 🌐 Floral Design Concept
Klaus Wagener
Dorothea Hamm

Floristik 🌐 Floral Design
Dorothea Hamm
Lena Lange
Klaus Wagener
Doreen Neumann
Michael Sutmöller

Fotos 🌐 Photography
Patrick Pantze Images GmbH, Lage (DE), www.patrick-pantze.de außer 🌐 except:
Seiten 🌐 pages 32–41: Robbert Beck (Gemeinschaftsproduktion mit 🌐 co-production with "Braut & Bräutigam")
Seiten 🌐 pages 42–45: Tina Fontana
Seiten 🌐 pages 84–85: Martina Herok, Harald Faber www.harald-faber.de

Grafik Design 🌐 Graphic Design
Riswane Abdurachmanov

DTP 🌐 DTP
Britta Baschen

BLOOM's
MEDIEN MARKETING EVENTS
WWW.BLOOMS.DE

Übersetzung 🌐 Translation
Jessica & Janet Brümmer, beyond words, Düsseldorf (D)

Druck 🌐 Print
D+L Printpartner GmbH, Bocholt (D)

Einzelbezugspreise 🌐 Single issue prices
„BLOOM's VIEW Wedding" erscheint 1 x im Jahr 🌐 "BLOOM's VIEW Wedding" is published once a year

Deutschland 🌐 Germany:
34,90 € inkl. MwSt. zzgl. Versand

Auslandspreise auf Anfrage
🌐 international prices upon request

Abo-Bezugspreise 🌐 Subscription prices
inkl. Versand 🌐 shipping included

Deutschland 🌐 Germany:
34,90 € inkl. MwSt. 🌐 incl. VAT

Schweiz 🌐 Switzerland:
48,90 SFR

sonstiges Europa 🌐 other European countries:
38,60 € exkl. MwSt. 🌐 excl. VAT

Übersee 🌐 overseas:
44,90 €

weitere Informationen unter 🌐 more information at www.blooms.de/view/abo

Abokündigungen bis 6 Wochen vor Erscheinen der Folgeausgabe jederzeit möglich. 🌐 Subscriptions can be cancelled anytime up to 6 weeks before publication of the next issue.

Ausgabe 🌐 issue: April 2017

Druckauflage 🌐 print run: 5 200

Hersteller und Produktnachweise 🌐 Manufacturers and products

ASA
www.asa-selection.de

BROSTE
www.brostecopenhagen.com

BUCO
www.buco-wire.com

D&M DEPOT
www.dmdepot.be

DIJK
www.dijknaturalcollections.com

DUTZ Collection
www.dutz.nl

FINK
www.fink-living.de

FREESE
www.heinr-freese.de

GASPER
www.gasper.de

GOLDINA
www.goldina.de

KARDELEN
www.kardelen.se

KFF
www.kff.de

KLOCKE
www.klocke-online.de

LEHNER
www.lehnerwolle3.com

LEONARDO
www.leonardo.de

MY ETAGERE
www.myetagere.ch

OASIS
www.oasisfloral.com

SERAX
www.serax.com

WABENBALL-SHOP
www.wabenball-shop.de

WENZEL
www.wenzel-kerzen.de

ZWIESEL
www.zwiesel-kristallglas.com

Danke 🌐 Thank you

Wir danken folgenden Personen dafür, dass sie sich als Models zur Verfügung stellten 🌐 We would like to thank the following individuals who posed as models in our photos:

Katrin Hartmann, Anja Hellner, Jaqueline Janzen, Jeliessa Juchler, Carina Kaatze, Malin Kaatze, Nele Marin, Christine Matern, Daniel Matern, Sabrina Meyer, Florian Michael, Paula Mohnke, Laura Orlob, Anja Oßenbrink, Jan Hendrik Rathert, Anna Reckeweg, Katharina Redecker, Darya Schwier, Katharina Seidel, Clara Stuhldreier, Franziska Wagener, Alina Wendland, Julian Winterberg sowie den Models von 🌐 as well as the models of "Braut & Bräutigam": Florence, Julia, Miriam, Wieteke, Zoë

Wir danken folgenden Personen und Firmen für das Zurverfügungstellen von Produkten und Ausstattungen 🌐 We would like to thank the following individuals and companies for provision of products, equipment & props:

Marion Muck, Köln (D), www.marion-muck.de, für Brautkleider 🌐 for brides' dresses

Die Nascherei, Minden (D), www.dienascherei.de, für die Hochzeitstorte 🌐 for the wedding cake

Ford Meyer, Bad Oeynhausen (D), www.ford-meyer-bad-oeynhausen.de, für das Brautauto 🌐 for the wedding car

Barendsen Flowers, Aalsmeer (NL), www.barendsen.nl, für vielerlei Schnittblumen 🌐 for many cut flowers

Wir danken dafür, dass wir an folgendem Ort fotografieren durften 🌐 We express our thanks for the following location, where we were permitted to take our photos:

Kurpark Bad Oeynhausen (D)

IMPRESSUM